D1171413

YOUR BONES

By Cyril Bassington

 Gareth Stevens
PUBLISHING

Please visit our website, www.garethstevens.com. For a free color catalog of all our high-quality books, call toll free 1-800-542-2595 or fax 1-877-542-2596.

Library of Congress Cataloging-in-Publication Data

Bassington, Cyril, author.
 Your bones / Cyril Bassington.
     pages cm. — (Know your body)
 Includes bibliographical references and index.
 ISBN 978-1-4824-4453-7 (pbk.)
 ISBN 978-1-4824-4397-4 (6 pack)
 ISBN 978-1-4824-4435-3 (library binding)
 1. Bones—Juvenile literature. 2. Skeleton—Juvenile literature. 3. Human physiology—Juvenile literature. I. Title.
  QM101.B7 2017
  612.7'51—dc23
                                            2015021475

Published in 2016 by
Gareth Stevens Publishing
111 East 14th Street, Suite 349
New York, NY 10003

Designer: Andrea Davison-Bartolotta
Editor: Therese Shea

Photo credits: Cover, p. 1 Jupiterimages/Stockbyte/Thinkstock; pp. 3, 4, 6, 8, 10, 12, 14, 16, 18, 20, 22–24 Anna Frajtova/Shutterstock.com; p. 5 SCIEPRO/Getty Images; p. 7 StockLite/Shutterstock.com; p. 9 Vectomart/Shutterstock.com; p. 11 wavebreakmedia/Shutterstock.com; p. 13 decade3d - anatomy online/Shutterstock.com; p. 15 Lightspring/Shutterstock.com; p. 17 BSIP/UIG/Getty Images; p. 19 Sebastian Kaulitzki/Shutterstock.com; p. 21 Spotmatik Ltd/Shutterstock.com.

Printed in the United States of America

CPSIA compliance information: Batch #CW16GS: For further information contact Gareth Stevens, New York, New York at 1-800-542-2595.

CONTENTS

Boldface words appear in the glossary.

Beautiful Bones

You're lucky you have bones. Without them, you couldn't stand or move. You would be a pile of skin and body parts. Yuck! The group of bones that make up the human body is called the skeletal system.

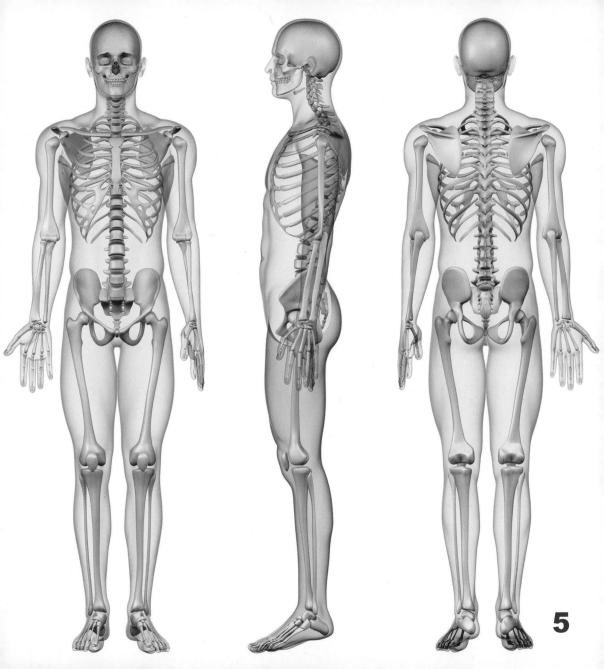

5

Did you know babies have about 300 bones when they're born? The bones grow bigger and longer each year. Some grow together. Your bones will be fully grown when you're about 25 years old. Adults have 206 bones.

In the Bones

Bones have many **layers**. In the middle of many bones is a thick matter called bone marrow. Bone marrow makes blood cells. The body needs blood cells for many reasons, including fighting illnesses and carrying **oxygen**.

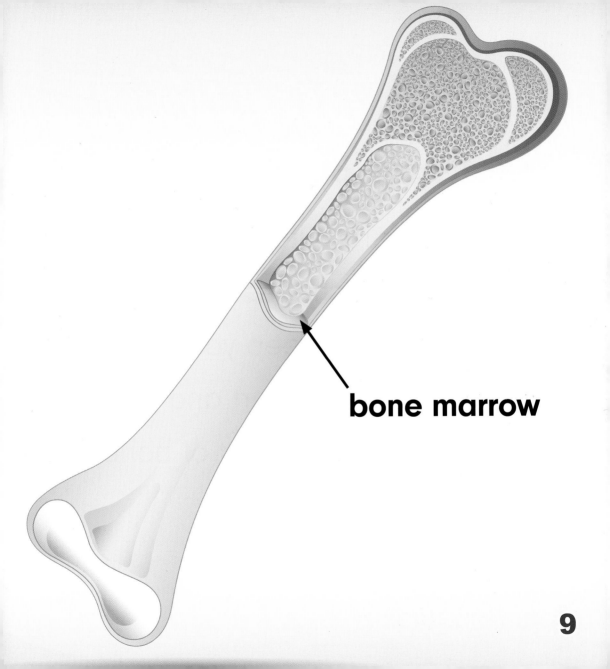

bone marrow

Meet Your Bones

Bones are hard but light. They give your body shape. Bones are strong enough to keep your soft **organs** safe. Your heart and lungs are found behind the set of bones called the rib cage.

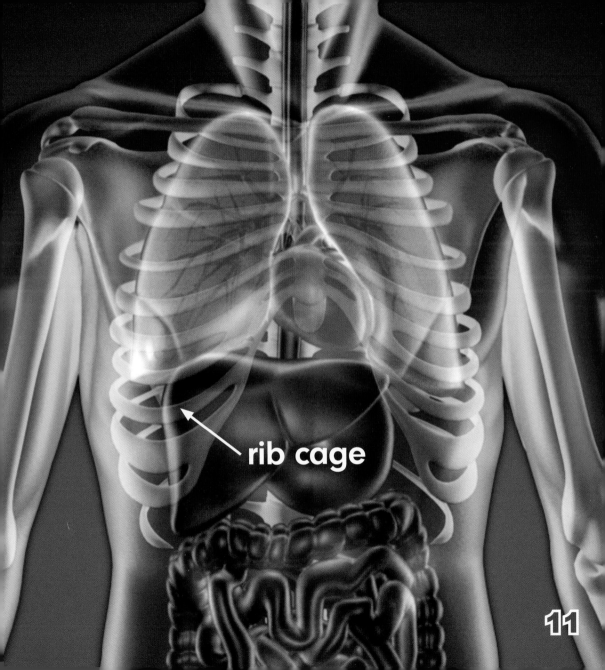

rib cage

11

It takes many bones working together to make up some parts of your body. The bones of your head are called the skull. The cranium is the part of the skull that protects, or guards, your brain.

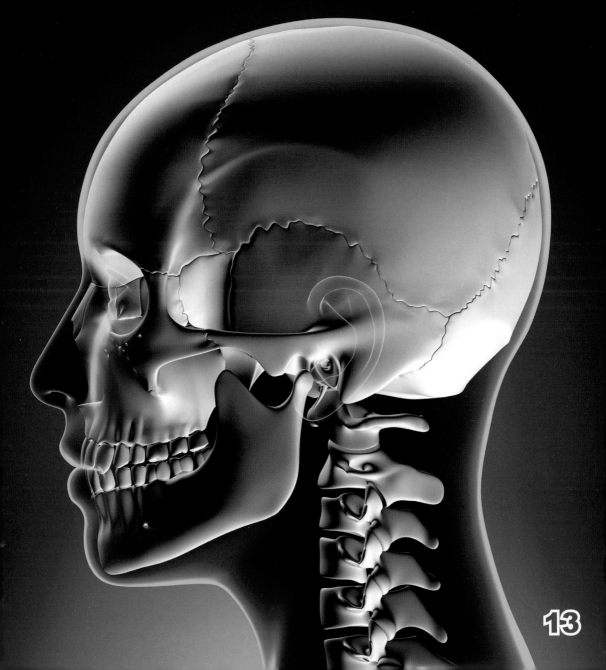

13

Your spine is in the center of your back. You can feel its bumps on the back of your neck. Your spine holds you up, but it lets you twist and bend down, too. Twenty-six bones make up the spine.

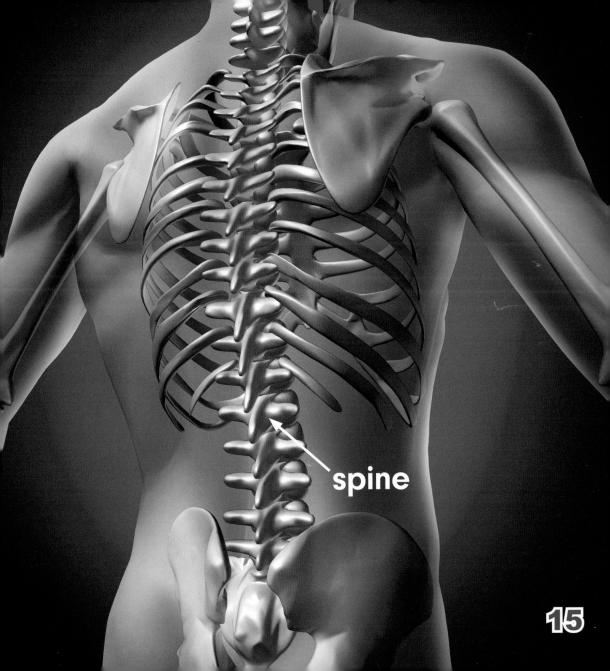

spine

15

Your arm is made up of three bones. The humerus (HYOO-muh-ruhs) is above your elbow. The radius and ulna are below the elbow. Your wrists, hands, and fingers are made up of 54 bones in all!

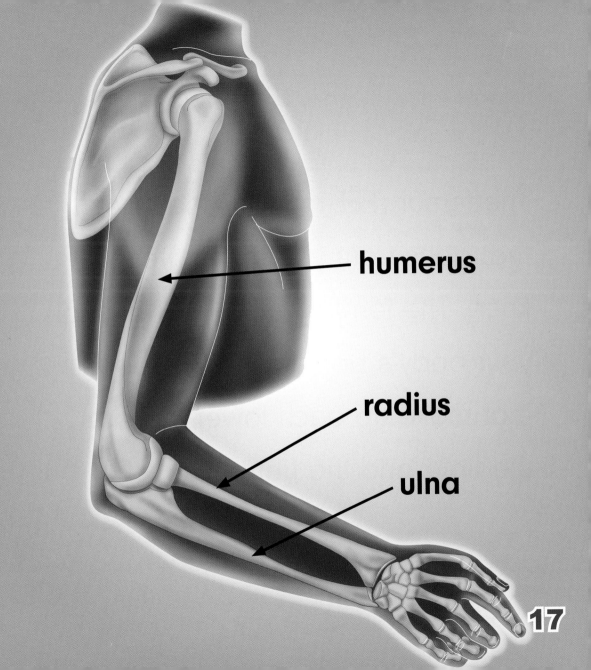

humerus

radius

ulna

17

The femur (FEE-muhr) is the bone that goes from your hip to your knee. The femurs are the longest of your body's bones. The two bones that make up each lower leg are the tibia and the fibula.

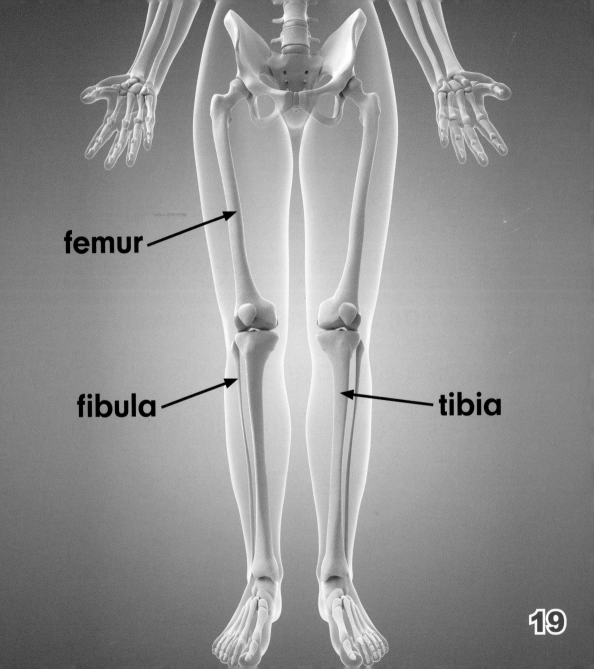

femur

fibula

tibia

19

Helping Your Bones

You can do things to keep your bones healthy. To keep your skull safe, wear a helmet when you're on a bike or playing sports such as football. Exercise and drink milk to keep your bones strong. Be good to your bones!

GLOSSARY

layer: one thickness of something lying over or under another

organ: a part inside a body that has a job to do

oxygen: a colorless gas that many animals, including people, need to breathe

FOR MORE INFORMATION

BOOKS

Cleland, Joann. *Why Do I Have Bones?* Vero Beach, FL: Rourke Publishing, 2009.

Rotner, Shelley, and David A. White. *Body Bones.* New York, NY: Holiday House, 2014.

Taylor, Lauren. *My Strong Bones.* Mankato, MN: QEB Publishing, 2013.

WEBSITES

Skeleton and Bone Facts
www.sciencekids.co.nz/sciencefacts/humanbody/skeletonbones.html
Read fun facts about your bones.

Your Bones
kidshealth.org/kid/htbw/bones.html
Find out much more about your amazing bones.

INDEX